RELIQUARIES

James Compton Bockmier

RELIQUARIES

James Compton Bockmier

threshpress
St. Louis, MO U.S.A.

Thresh Press
St. Louis, MO 63011

Acknowledgements

"The Rock," "Ready to Burst," and "Babel" first appeared in
In Black + White, Art Meets Writing, 2nd Edition,
Exhibition Catalog, SAA Collective, 2018.
Reprinted by permission of the author.

"Aeolic Hymn" first appeared in *Activator, the Art Issue,* Issue 30,
December 2020. Reprinted by permission of the author

Source art for the cover created by
James T. Elliot

Manufactured in the United States of America

ISBN: 978-0-578-75328-7

threshpress
St. Louis, MO U.S.A.

CONTENTS

FOREWORD

BY ETHAN LEWIS

A preface to this collection can serve its purpose best by referring the reader to James Bockmier's own "Foreword." Rarely does one come upon a poet so conscientious, comprehensive, and accurate about what he has wrought. Even so, to supplement his apercu, I can elaborate — e.g., by extending remarks about prosody ("us[ing] freedom from templates" to augment effects *through* rhyme and meter[1]) to compass spatial forms. Like a sculptor, Bockmier often incorporates space as part-and-parcel of the whole:

> The door is narrow
>
> And ego's immensity
>
> Cannot fit the frame.
>
> Leave it at the coat-check room;
>
> Your truest friend waits within.

The obvious mimetic shortening of the lines sets the verbal scene for more subtle, *enactive* effects. The second line's length exceeds that of the first, and, isochronous with the third, forms one-half of a semantic equation: the outsized ego is synonymous with exceeding the frame. The fourth line functions as gatekeeper, separating the condition depicted above from the company "within": genuinely situated beyond/under "the coat-check room." "Your truest friend," the self dis-encumbered from the heavy, suffocating garment—and moreover, the *truest* self: Polonius waxed fatuously that "the apparel oft proclaims the man" (*Ham.* I.iii.72); "why do you dress me In borrowed robes?" Macbeth queried (*Macb.* I.iii.108—requires subtraction by addition, attained via augmented line length comprising the imperative to "Leave it"; and yielding a new isochronous semantic synonymity. Checking the appurtenant ego at the door equates with becoming the truest friend in the room beyond.

It may be protested that critical over-ingenuity here merely masquerades as an ingenious poem. But that objection, more than discounting Bockmier's *expressed* modesty in another verse pensée:

> Lest I proudly preach
> Humility, I preach it
> Firstly to myself.
>
> I speak not as one humble,
> But as one who seeks to be.

—also fails to take into account his fundamental assumption, which coordinates poetics with spiritual workings: "the striving [of the poet or the auditor] has an independent value deriving from the holy rather than from us. May you bring this striving to these poems as they bring it to you." Bockmier would concur with Auden that "Poetry makes nothing happen"; poetry, rather, constitutes "a way of happening"[2] through creative interaction.

To continue this supplementary elaboration upon Bockmier's auto-exegesis. The poet's "care and joy in the most delicate...constructions of form" may comprise a "celebratory" display of "primarily aural effects (assonance, alliteration, etc.)": at times in conjunction with subject matter:

> From these great welling floods flows new,
>
> Lush interlace. Jazz grows, *swims*.
>
> Modern music hits tones likewise weaving.
>
> And thus the circle turns.

—or alternately, the festive is predicated on "word play, parallelism, and any other rhetorical figures I can dig up [troweling chiasmus in what follows]":

> My love, as now I lie upon death's door,
>
> I know I shall find
>
> You in God hereafter,
>
> As I have found God in you here before.

In either case — in all cases — the *reliquaries* prove "celebratory[, e]ven when the poem is not happy — even when it is outright and crushingly tragic." Poignant case in point: "Elegy for Jake Malone," occasioned by a *genuinely* crushing end:

> Your body jumped
> And wrenched the Spirit from the matter
> Needlessly.

Yet the cinematic genius who conferred release from (and the obsessive diction mimes the state) "my glaring pretense of self-preoccupation"; who "brought me outside myself," is preserved in a kindred medium. In effect, the elegist rescues in turn; or rather, assists in the retrieval by raising to the surface Malone's undying flame:

> The chemicals that failed to nourish
> Cannot drown you.
> The killing that could not save you
> Cannot kill your saving.
> You are as you have ever been;
> The Queenedom of Faerie is within.

Two matters of note: 1.) As much in message, the poem's celebratory air consists in word play and sound scheme; to poach from Pound's lexicon, in *logopoeia* ("the dance of the intellect with words") and *melopoeia* ("inducing emotional correlations by sound." Though in Bockmier there is much for the mind's eye — *phanopoeia* — the audial and witful prove his chief means of "charging language with meaning."[3]) Even lexicography (*phanopoeia* of a sort) — "Queen*e*dom of F*ae*rie" — partakes in the solemnity (— for rightly construed, high celebration is *solempne*. Cf. C.S. Lewis: "The *Solempne* is the festal which is also the stately and the ceremonial"[4]. From the "Foreword": "Poetry is celebratory as a priest celebrates a mass.") Yet stately exuberance is chiefly rendered via the triumphant turn from "killing that could not save" to "Cannot kill your saving"; and by the joyful noise of the concluding couplet: the sole rhyme in the piece. Regarding which, we can tinker a bit with the syntax in the "Foreword": "I use my freedom from templates to employ *rhyme more*." A late verse in *reliquaries* likewise aptly glosses:

> Whereas writing songs
> Puts words to music
> So as then to sing the words,

Writing poetry

Puts music IN the words

So that the words themselves may sing.

R.P. Blackmur, similarly, described poetry as "behavior that gets
into our language and sings."[5]

2.) "Elegy for Jake Malone" intimates the "fundamentally
Neo-Platonic" note that prevails throughout this collection,
prefacing which Bockmier specifies. Thus, the elegizing devotee
can but contribute to the restoration of his idol because any single
action — every discrete thing — proves one of myriad emanations
from a divine, predicative One. The initial verse in *reliquaries*
trumpets the theme:

Any one thing is all others,

Only at a given angle of approach.

Set aside the accidental,

Incidental, all excrescence,

Leaving bare the presence,

Original essence,

Crystal-cut space-free geometry

Of Platonic ideal purity.

The prolonged lyric catechism "In Myself" rings variations on this notion, in quatrain after quatrain — some of those more notable follow:

I am not

A thing in need

But rather

Need itself.

*

I am not

A thing contingent.

Contingency

Itself I be.

*

The contingent

Is the shadow

Of the

Necessary Being.

*

The effect

Is none but

The very

Causal relation.

*

The effect

Is causedness

In relation

To the cause.

*

In itself

Being is

Verily

The Necessary.

Only in Its

Self-Disclosures

Do Its

Determinations vary.

In itself

Existence is

Verily

The One,

All else but

Shadows,

Manifestations,

Rays of the Sun.

The cadenced setting of these koans lends to the impression of their truth.

Coincident with the featured doctrine — or, in the light of its precepts, *coalescent*, Bockmier's largescale design. His division into "forecourt" and "sanctuary" appears modeled upon George Herbert's demarcation of "The Church Porch" from "The Church" proper in his monumental *The Temple* (1633)[6] — which, with Donne's oeuvre, Shakespeare's *Sonnets* and *The Phoenix and the Turtle*, constitutes the lyric zenith of a Golden Age. Yet in *reliquaries* no partition is erected, nor hardly pertains. How telling that in the "Foreword" "sanctuary" is mentioned *before* "forecourt" (a decision seemingly purposeful as Bockmier's wider spacing between lines):

> The poems in "sanctuary" deal with the core philosophical-cum-spiritual themes grounding my poetic practice, and indeed my life and thought generally. The poems in "forecourt" meanwhile classify as light or occasional verse. These are not separate, nor is the material in "forecourt" a mere afterthought, even as the themes in "sanctuary" enjoy absolute precedence. Indeed, it is precisely because of this absolute precedence that the themes in "sanctuary"

spill over into — and then reassimilate to themselves — the themes of "forecourt."

"The effect is causedness in relation to the cause." "Spill over" is instanced, e.g., by segueing the light-hearted "Rusillo," which still *celebrates* this

> Workingman's superman seeking
> To impede a greed stampede
> Of plutocratic pachyderms,
> A labor of love born of a love of labor

— into a most somber meditation on "Primeval fratricidal appetites Driv[ing] Our ever advancing engines of destruction." Though nevertheless, "A Theodicy" concludes on a "Rusillo"-esque playful affirmation that turns a conventional cynicism on its head:

> In the vastness of our cosmos,
> Some monkeys type Shakespeare.
> A sonnet's emergence from truly large numbers
> Absolves our evolution.

So goes a "reassimilation" of "forecourt" into "sanctuary." So shall the reader likewise find many a splendid emanation of the poetic One comprised by *reliquaries*.

Notes

1.) These prosodic intentions correspond with Eliot. Cf. "Reflections on *Vers Libre*" (1917): "The ghost of some simple metre should lurk behind the arras in even the 'freest' verse; to advance menacingly as we doze, and withdraw as we rouse....[L]iberation from rhyme might be as well a liberation of rhyme. Freed from its exacting task of supporting lame verse, it could be applied with greater effect where it is most needed. There are often passages in an unrhymed poem where rhyme is wanted for some special effect, for a sudden tightening up or a cumulative insistence, or for an abrupt change in mood." (T.S. Eliot, *"To Criticize the Critic and Other Writings"* [Lincoln: U of Nebraska P, 1965], 187, 189.)

2.) W.H. Auden, "In Memory of W.B. Yeats," II.

3.) "How to Read" (1929), *Literary Essays of Ezra Pound*, ed. T.S. Eliot (New York: New Directions, 1968), 25.

4.) C.S. Lewis, *A Preface to Paradise Lost* (1942; rpt. London: Oxford, 1969), 17.

5.) "Lord Tennyson's Scissors," R.P. Blackmur, *Language as Gesture* (New York: Columbia UP, 1952), 488.

6.) Bockmier embraces a wide-ranging and eclectic array of influences, always utilized in modes distinctly his own. More prevalent than others 'mongst the echoed: Skelton,

Spenser, the Bard, various Blues artists and rappers, Keats, Poe, and Vachel Lindsay. My first exchange with James concerned Ben Jonson. Yet the seventeenth century sensibility most closely approximating his may belong to Henry Vaughan. They share in mystic wonder. Cf., e.g., in rhythm as well as sentiment

> Last night a dreamt I saw the Trinity,
> My imagination seeing clear.
> I can't remember how Divinity
> In shape or tone or color then appeared.
> Be that as it may, I think
> That even as I woke I knew
> I saw each person real and quite distinct
>
> ....

With

> I saw eternity the other night
> Like a great ring of pure and endless light,
>   All calm as it was bright;
> And round beneath it, time, in hours, days, years,
>   Driven by the spheres,
> Like a vast shadow moved, in which the world
>   And all her train were hurled.

INTRODUCTION:

AN ARS POETICA

I have liked to think of my favorite poetic creations as "little jewel boxes." I take care and joy in the most delicate, most elaborate, and most dazzling constructions of form. This is celebratory. Even when the poem is not happy — even when it is outright and crushingly tragic — it is still celebratory. It is celebratory as a priest celebrates a mass. Poetry is a spiritual exercise for me and I take up its practice with the awesome gravity of a holy vocation. It is in light of my little jewel boxes' role in holy service that I have further termed them — and this volume — *reliquaries*.

I have divided this collection into two main sections: "sanctuary" and "forecourt." The poems in "sanctuary" deal with the core philosophical-cum-spiritual themes grounding my poetic practice, and indeed my life and thought generally. The poems in "forecourt" meanwhile classify as light or occasional verse. These are not separate, nor is the material in "forecourt" a mere afterthought, even as the themes in "sanctuary" enjoy absolute precedence. Indeed, it is precisely because of this absolute precedence that the themes in "sanctuary" spill over into — and then reassimilate to themselves — the themes of forecourt. As an architectural metaphor, "sanctuary" is the core sacred space in a house of worship while forecourt is the public space (marketplace, town square, etc.) gathering together worldly activity and ultimately offering it before a higher calling.

The underlying philosophy my poems express is fundamentally Neo-Platonic. At least in this regard my poems do not represent a dramatic persona (though some may in other respects) but rather my real thought. I have employed terminology and imagery from a variety of world religious, intellectual, and mythological traditions in the process of communicating this philosophy. This is no accident as the traditions in question were under Neo-Platonic influence (Sufism, Catholicism) or exhibited some strong Neo-Platonic parallels (Vedanta, Taoism, Zen).

The form of my writing is unabashedly decorative and formal, even Marinistic. Though I only occasionally employ fixed forms, I use my freedom from templates to employ more rhyme and meter, not less. Namely, I can employ more complex rhyme patterns and rhythmic shifts when I need not use a single meter and rhyme scheme throughout. Along with these and other primarily aural effects (assonance, alliteration, etc.), I make copious use of word play, parallelism, and any other rhetorical figures I can dig up.

I do not see the combination of philosophical mysticism and decorative formalism as merely incidental. While neither per se requires the other, I do find them most naturally suited to combination. Formalism illustrates the "abstract" character of such mysticism while decorative profusion reflects that such is not "mere" abstraction in the nominalist sense (such nominalism being precisely the primary object of opposition) but an inexhaustible wealth of active potentiality.

It is with these words of introductory explanation that I invite you to open my little jewel boxes. Moreover, and most of all, open yourself to the sacred. Whichever spiritual tradition you may operate out of, or if you operate independently, I hope you may find in my poems something of the universal striving for the holy. Bumbling as my own personal striving may often be, the striving has an independent value deriving from the holy rather than from us. May you bring this striving to these poems and may they bring it to you.

SANCTUARY

Aeolic Hymn

Oh, great Lord! Heaven's Light!

    See the sun's gold orb emit your wisdom,

    the light of lights!

Oh, great Lord! Heaven's Light!

    You give the saints prophetic sight,

    witness of truth in truth.

Oh, great Lord! Heaven's Light!

    You bid the chariot come spread philosophy afar.

Oh, great Lord! Heaven's Light!

    Finger hitting strings of the lyre,

    you give us sounds of song.

Oh, great Lord! Heaven's Light!

    Lift up my song,

    through love of wisdom's inner sight,

    to life in light!

Honesty

Honesty is a habit

Drenched in danger

Far in excess of narcotics.

How mild the risks of heroin

Next to those of heroines and heroes

Speaking truth to power.

Messengers shot up with arrows

Are fleshy pin cushions —

St. Sebastian's living icons.

Though, rest assured,

Angels without number

Will dance atop each arrow-pin

In circling celebration

Of each newly re-born martyr's

Final apotheosis.

Any one thing is all others,

Only at a given angle of approach.

Set aside the accidental,

Incidental, all excrescence,

Leaving bare the presence,

Original essence,

Crystal-cut space-free geometry

Of Platonic ideal purity.

Inquantum

Existence exists
And I exist, too.
Existence, I have
My Being through You!

Alone, You exist,
Uncomposite One!
Where does that leave me,
Oh planet-less Sun?

If I do exist,
Alone you can't be.
If you are alone,
There can't be a me.

Unless we are one,
Identical, same,
Distinctions confined
To level of name.

My limits, imperfect,
Are foreign to This
Transfinite All-Real
Which perfectly is.

Yet bracket my faults,
No longer does there
Appear any split
Between our affairs.

As per all my faults,
I'm nothing but null.
So far as I'm real,
I'm You then in full.

Mine eyes have seen the glory

Of the coming of the Lord,

Its coming and its going,

During, after, and before,

Every single instant,

For God all instants one,

God the single instant

From whence all instants sprung.

There is nothing else to see

But the glory of the Lord.

I set to dive into Shiva's third eye

That I may annihilate myself in his Being.

Only, I annihilate Lord Shiva —

    No longer distinct from Lord Vishnu,

    Nor from servant-creatures —

Leaving Brahman without distinctions.

Only none annihilates any;

    Only Brahman ever is,

    One without part or second.

I am that.

Thou art that.

My friend the wise woman once suggested,

Rather than a spiritual battle contested,

Seeing my inner life though another analogy;

Understand my work as polishing a mirror

To see myself and the world clearer.

To fight oneself and seek to smite

Some inner blight and make things right

Makes one two, the one against the other, though each the self.

What use slaying self if self must do the slaying?

If any is to remain, the self must do the staying.

Only, we mistake the self for the grime upon the glass.

Shine the silvery surface; see it reflect all that pass.

Reflections do not alter a spotless mirror's substance.

It accepts all forms and binds to none,

Within itself remaining one.

Even dust and tarnish cannot breach the mirror's core.

Polish the self and see the same sheen as before.

Wipe down any surface anywhere and likewise see the same,

A self not merely mine or yours,

      but the single spark in each and all,

The world in Blake's grain of sand, the great within the small.

This inner-beyond endured intact all ravages of civil strife

Raging about my psyche for roughly half my life.

My struggle was honest, even valiant,

      but nigh satirically absurd.

Force of arms cannot win a goodness not first mine.

Yet polishing the mirror I find an inmost goodness shine.

The Divine does not so much

Give to us ourselves

As lend Itself   to us.

The Divine does not

Create new being,

      Distinct although dependent,

And then bestow such being

To be ours and as such be us.

Rather the Divine IS Being,

      Being being the Divine.

Only Being ever is

      And yet is

      In any and all

      And thus in us,

And by Being being in us

      (though never truly ours)

We, as such, are.

At the center of the intelligible cosmos

    Of ordered worlds

    And worlds within these,

Amidst concentric hosts —

    Of purple, green, and orange —

    Sounding chords,

And then a second triad —

    Red, blue, and yellow —

    Giving forth clear tones,

Sits an opal

    Circling with

    The infinitesimal arabesque

    Omni-polyrhythmic fugue of fugues,

And at its center —

    The center —

    Is the space-less all-dense point

    Of deafening quiet.

Last night I dreamt I saw the Trinity,

My imagination seeing clear.

I can't remember how Divinity

In shape or tone or color then appeared.

Be that as it may, I think

That even as I woke I knew

I saw each person real and quite distinct —

A single God, though I forget its hue.

What symbols then I saw for that which eyes can't pierce

Presently elude my memory.

However, neither dove nor man nor cross came near

The metaphor that came to visit me.

I saw no feathered tail and no white wing.

From what my power to recall allows,

It seemed a very abstract sort of thing,

No bastard trinity of stones or cows.

I still see Oneness with no trace of multiplicity

Transcending each distinction of the three.

Indeed, I both imagine and quite frankly hope

That this will be the way I always see.

Yet need these visions contradict?

I hope not and no longer see

Absurdity as following

Affirming them both simultaneously.

Holy Saturday: Eclipse of the Son

When

    (as Athanasias said)

"The impassible suffered" —

    Going down to harrow hell

    For to deliver Moses and his kin

        Across the final pass,

The intelligible orb

(without circumference, and center omnipresent)

    In its filial person

    Suffered no diminution,

        But passed from mortal view

        So as to pass us through

        And deliver mortals to

        Beatific vision.

Elegy for Jake Malone

He leapt and plunged from a bridge.

The impact hit me reading the news.

We, the living, endure

To process the remains.

Broken down, though brilliant,

He broke himself into the ground;

In my glaring pretence of self-preoccupation,

I think how I hurt from it.

Only, his films brought me outside myself,

Outside daily doing this so as to do that,

Into darkly luminous fairyland

Of jumping bodies

Jumping out their matter into Spirit.

Jake Malone,

Your body jumped

And wrenched the Spirit from the matter

Needlessly.

Countless times prior

You jumped into your Spirit.

The Queenedom of Faerie is within!

And, whether you knew or no,

All those damned chemicals were superfluous.

You unto yourself hold the black magic bitchcraft

And your powers need no potions.

Your death—

The closing and cataclysmic superfluity.

Spirit no more needs body's death than it needs body.

Self-complete, no different

In body's death or life,

Spirit embraces no less the fairyland.

The chemicals that failed to nourish

Cannot drown you.

The killing that could not save you

Cannot kill your saving.

You are as you have ever been;

The Queenedom of Faerie is within.

Cigar

Each and any object of itself

Opens up an infinite expanse,

An interior omni-comprehensive

All-origin all-in-all

From each to each and back again,

Only ever as it is, as same self.

A cigar is significant as cigar,

Not "just cigar"

As though a tawdry trifle.

A given cigar so far surpasses

Being but a roll of leaf husks.

Husks are but preliminaries

To embodiment where and when

Cigar-essence

Condenses, crystallizes

Ambient aromas,

Almost origami,

Enfolding papers

Into dense, efficient forms

Potent for fiery release

Of energy now mass.

The root rules of matter's motion

Lie in one cigar.

So too do the principles

Of unity's ontology,

    Complicatio et explicatio,

    Enfolding and unfolding.

A cigar is all this in itself,

Everything all at once in each.

Nature is itself superlative,

Nature not as this or that

    — here and now or there and then —

But of each and all the nature

Of what it is

To be.

Taking fairy tale for physical fact
Forces fairy into corporeal frame
Unfit for delicate wings.

Forgoing fairyland
Removes truth from fact
—no longer even that—
Now mere, sheer physical form.

Shun sham science of religion.
Shun sham religion of science.
Find fairy's true formless form
Beyond, before the physical.

Like little Belgium but a century before,

      I sit between the hostile   roar

      Of two established powers.

Though for me these be not France and Prussia,

      But a pair of strong-willed women

      With those their wills

      Set crossed in combat.

The one, she seeks to serve

      As sword in God's right hand;

The other blares a march to march to

      In quest for modern progress.

I for my part sit and seek a quiet peace

      Within the Little Way,

That I may find and share the little flower

      Our Lord offers from the left.

I am the All-Author's immediate word,

    Bypassing pen and paper's intervention,

    The direct expression

    Of inner silence remaining

        Even as it proceeds.

To be at all is already to express the All-Author,

    From Author's own pure being —

        Intrinsically, effortlessly

        Self-expressing —

    To prime matter's

        Mere potential to express.

Though, without exception,

We are words within the universal book,

    Our calling is to be the book —

        Not only word in the world

        But the world in oneself,

        The holy writ in whole.

I am Your Act,

Not just Your effect.

From Your Dominion

I cannot defect.

No independence

Have I whatsoever.

I am Your Act.

I am Your Endeavor.

I am Your Doing,

Your Deed and Your Word.

I am Your seen.

I am Your heard.

Yet also I am

Your hearing, Your Seeing;

Lacking my own,

I share in Your Being,

Not as Your partner,

Nor as Your part,

Yet as Your Craft

And as Your Art.

Like fallen Adam, ashamed of his nakedness,

    I face its Origin

In prayer without liturgy

    Robing or clothing my soul,

Only bare presence before the One —

    Or rather only the One can be present,

      One without second

          (e.g. me-qua-me).

No wonder finitude's anxiety!

Form of prayer

      — petition, praise, and so forth

      (always mine of the Other) —

      Cocoons me still in me-ness

         Oblivious

         To chrysalis'

      Death of me-ness

      And birth to unborn, undying me-less Self.

A Theodicy

We are a race of nuclear-capable chimps.

As we hoot and scratch,

The red button lies within our reach.

How did it come to this?

Four billion years of living

While siblings die —

The tree of life's growing

Limbs and broken boughs.

Primeval fratricidal appetites

Drive bodies in the billions,

Driving in their turn

Our ever advancing engines of destruction.

Only, bio-destiny's blight

Misses certain minute branches

Where fragile, fragrant blossoms spring.

In the vastness of our cosmos,

Some monkeys type Shakespeare.

A sonnet's emergence from truly large numbers

Absolves our evolution.

No Greater Poverty

No poverty is greater
Than ownership's illusion:
"My life," "my body,"
"My possessions,"

To be a petty tyrant
With no greater purpose,
Lording over
Utter insignificance,

To reign in hell,
An endless void of
An isolated individual's
Creaturely nothingness.

Dispelling illusion
Unveils the wealth of knowing
That others are our self.
We owe our-self to serve.

Meditation: A Meditation

I place myself in holy presence,
Wholly at divine disposal.

I lock my mind and limbs
In floriate petal composition,
Up-flaming free and clean as lotus.

My mind-body but a statue mold
     Breaking after filled with gold,
A gleaming tangerine ore
     In yoga form,
Only for the Golden One
     To break my ego-idol,
Melt me and imbibe me back
     To origin I forgot I never left.

Rationalism Contra Empiricism

What cannot be is not;
Damn if your eyes
> Say otherwise.

What's more, they're mute.
> EYES
> SAY nothing.

What cannot not be is;
> If you fail to see it,
> The failure lies with sight.
Only mind can know.

Dis-Confirmation

Years ago I sold my soul,

Perjured myself upon an altar,

Swore to what I wished was so

But knew that it was not.

Years since I claimed my karmic debt,

Mortified upon a cross of Truth

My will to believe in a cross of Christ—

Or rather willfulness of feigned belief.

Still, integrity's recovery

Could not restore an innocence

Most had long since lost.

I repent "growing up."

Public Prayer

Neither cede I
    Right to
    Public prayer,
Nor cede I
    Public prayer
    To the right;

Meditating on a park bench,
    I shout my quiet to the rooftops.

Prepare to praise God

      For your own

      Damnation.

Though if you be so ready,

Then no such day shall come.

*

Those who believe

Only what they see

Can never believe

A symphony.

*

Thy Hand doth sweep 'cross land and sea.

'Tween peak and bay near-corpses move,

But slight they move; once warm, now freeze.

Thy Hand forgets not death and tomb.

In myself

I am

Nothing,

A non-entity,

A phantom,

Unreality,

A vacuum,

A void.

In myself

I do not

Exist.

Neither do you.

Only He is

In Himself.

He is

The True.

The whole of

My reality,

In its whole

Totality,

Is none

But my

Modality

Vis a vis Him.

My being

Is none but

My need for

His sacred Grace.

Everything

Doth perish

But for

His sacred Face.

He did not

Create for me

A being

Of my own.

Rather, through

My locus

His Light

Doth proudly shone.

He does not
Sustain for me
A being
Of my own.

Rather, all
I am is
But the glow
From His Throne.

No separate
Identity
May I
Truly claim.

Of any
Independence
May I say
The same.

I am not
An entity,
Only a
Relation.

Such is the
Lowliness
Of my
Wretched station.

My very
Definition
Is in terms
Of Him.

His Light
Is intense,
My reflection
Of it dim.

I am but
My need for Him,
My poverty
Of being.

I am my
Contingency,
Such I am
Now seeing.

I am not

A thing in need

But rather

Need itself.

In myself

I am sickness.

His Light

Brings forth health.

I am not

A thing 'tis poor

But rather

Poverty.

I am not

A thing contingent.

Contingency

Itself I be.

I am not

A thing created.

Createdness

Itself I am.

Next to Him

Or His pure friends

My being is but

Shame and sham.

In itself

Being is

Verily

The Necessary.

Only in Its

Self-Disclosures

Do Its

Determinations vary.

In itself

Existence is

Verily

The One,

All else but

Shadows,

Manifestations,

Rays of the Sun.

In itself

Reality is

Verily

The Real.

Reality

By Itself exists.

It cannot possibly

Fail to be.

Before Him

Must we

Bow our heads

And ever, always kneel.

Such is

The proof

Of the

Sincere,

Images in

The mirror,

Waves upon

The Sea,

The inner

Prophet

Reason

They do hear.

That is all

At final count

Our relational

Realities be.

Such is

The proof

Of the

Veracious,

Existence

Necessarily is.

Being verily

Must be.

The honest

And the

Truthful

Gracious.

The contingent

Is the shadow

Of the

Necessary Being.

Verily such is

A Truth

Worth knowing and

Worth seeing.

The effect

Is none but

The very

Causal relation.

Such is its

Lowliness.

Such is its

Station.

The effect

Is causedness

In relation

To the cause.

Take note that such

Admonition

May give thee

Substantial pause.

For such

Indeed

Is the

True meaning

Of the

Gradation and

The Unity

Of Being.

Existence is

"Analogical,"

"Systematically

Ambiguous,"

Coming in

Intense and weak,

The more perfect

And the less.

At the "plane
Of Its Essence"
Being is perfect
In the Absolute,

Yet in Its
Relational
Manifestations
Comes forth a lesser suit.

The lesser
Grows more
And the more
More still,

On and on,
On until
Each existence
Eats its fill.

Its substance moves
Its essence quakes,
Indeed its very
Being shakes.

Substance moves,
Essence quakes,
Till each existence
Its perfection takes.

May praise
Be His
And fault
Be mine.

Glory to Him
Divine,
Blessed, and
All Sublime.

Spenserian Sonnet

The primal principle would be a point,
Except it has no need of any place
Locating it in relations (arc, joint,
Predication) in syntax, time or space.

Once placed the point begins to pulse and race.
From place springs space in motion crossing time.
The fast depart the slow as though in chase.
Through six directions color-tones prism and chime.

Around the primal point the swirls climb.
As notes make music so that shapes may dance,
Kaleidoscopic webs of forms combine.
Each form all other forms as one enhance.

From bare perfection these adornments come
And through that same perfection live as one.

Spenserian Stanza

> The Knight-Queen Sophia in gleaming arms
> Of steel rides steed and bears a shield bedight
> With emblem of four cardinals. Grave harms
> From foes and thorns beset, but armor bright
> And strong sets straight her will, the will her white
> Horse heeds impeccably. Undaunted, she
> Rides forth — and into dragon's keep; by right
> The holy grail she seeks. This hers shall be
> To wash her face, her steel, and steed at life's true tree.

Sophia at the Gate

You face a gate
>Giving open view and forward thrust
Unto a journey crossing vast lands
>—some parched, some verdant—
>Marked with perils and prizes.

Your figure,
>Hopefully-a-hero-in-the-making,
Summons forth my memory of being at this place
>In my time
>A one not so unlike you;
Indeed, you so reflect the best I recollect of my then-self,
>Even as from what I see my failings fall not on you.

The way is steep, deep and dangerous—
>Soul-forging fires
>And pressure pits for diamond minds—
But be not discouraged!
Take courage in your character as one well suited
>To suit up in brilliant armor
>And meet head on your challenge.

Tyrants of fortress-garrisons will seek enslaving

    You in your deeds, words, and very thoughts,

    Extinguishing virtues save for loyalty

      And transmuting this to vice —

      Vice of obeisance reft of vision.

Wild bands will seek to sweep you up

In aimless furor of dissipation and destruction

    That cannot but end in cannibalizing its own impulse.

Wisdom be thy name;

    Know this!

      Know the wisdom of the womb-queen

      Granting this name-boon as a birth-gift

      With the gift of birth!

"To thine own self be true"

And beyond this be true to Truth;

    Be not only true but indeed be Truth!

    For Widsom is Truth and thou art Wisdom!

Necessitarianism

The Self-Necessary of necessity necessitates —
And by necessitating all, all is necessarily so.
Necessity of no-need
        and necessity of need.
Necessity necessitating
        and necessity necessitated.
None but one necessity throughout.

What is to be?

      "Brute facts,"

      So say the brutes,

As though to be were this or that,

Though this need not be

      Nor need that.

Yet to be cannot but be.

Indeed, to be this or that

      Is not to be the other,

      To NOT be.

To be is not to not be but to be.

To be is all simply in so much

As all simply are,

Indifferent to difference,

Undifferentiated one-all.

"To be is God,"

"Esse est deus,"

So saith Meister Eckhart.

Higher Than Your Cross?

Do not hang, as some have,
Your flag and medals
Higher than your cross.

Or else, like some
(like so, so many),
You hang God's poorest children
Nailed with medals
To two flags
At right angles.

As for the least of us,
So too for him,
You hang Christ nailed up
Yet again.

Act for God,

Which is to act

For the least among us,

For or against country.

God blesses but the just;

God save US from US so to bless US,

Otherwise God damn US as is just.

The guiltless babe cries out

For likewise crying mother's arms

As they recede under duress

From agents of authority,

    Pursuant to the law

    They claim to constitute

    Their sacred duty.

Did the Roman solider

    Driving nails through flesh and bone

Do his duty as would since

    Be Christians' sacred duty to the law?

Did the Holy Family sin in flight

> To Egypt

> Made in haste and fright

> Of Herod's infant massacre?

Did Mary fail to render unto Caesar

> Via Herod?

> Was Christ

> His, not hers?

Tearing babe from loving mother

Tears the Son of Man

From Heaven's Mother.

Having as it seems

Now stolen out

Our prizest season Spring,

Which wonders from

John's Revelation

Will the hidden wealthy ones

Next bring forth to pass?

A politician is indeed,

With but rare exception,

But a whore of Babylon.

Like H.G. Wells,

It tempts me for

My epitaph to read

"God damn you all!

I told you so."

Only, God but keeps our karma.

With algebraic justice

Detached from wrath,

God damns those who damn themselves.

Martyr Ballad

Sing, oh sing, this ballade strong

Of Joseph, martyr of Ctesiphon.

He gave his life for Jesus Christ,

His Heavenly Father, and the Fire-Tongued Geist.

"God is One," said Joseph martyr.

"From the truth this could not be farther,"

Said the Magian heathen, Mobed rabid,

Before to death he Joseph martyr stabbed.

The heathen said, "God is two! God is two!"

Joseph martyr said, "You know full well this is not true.

You tell this to the workmen and the peasants small

That you may more easily collect cruel taxes come the Fall."

"Ah, so worse than a heretic or even apostate,

You challenge the power of our Shah and State!"

The Mobed shouted, frothing at his devilish mouth,

"Long live the Shah, East to West and North to South!"

"Indeed long live the Shah,

    and may his reign be Just,

In One God in three persons

    may our monarch trust,"

Said Joseph, only further angering the Mobed,

    who went on to plea,

"You said your God is One,

    then just now you say God's Three!"

"By the two great Gods, I ask,

    where lies your reason should you be sane?"

Joseph replied, "God lies beyond my reason,

    upon the very highest plane.

Here blessed indetermination rules,

    with no distinction between One and Three,

Undifferentiated and non-numerical,

    the two are a single simple Trinity."

"Ah, now you admit God to be two,"

    said the Mobed with an evil grin,

"Now deny He's three and that He's One,

    and I might let you free again!

Providing, that is, you make an oath

    to be ever and always loyal,

To everything Zorastrian, Magian,

    Persian and first and foremost royal."

"God is indeed two in some sense,

    but also three, and first and foremost One,"

Said Joseph, "Yet distinct, different,

    or separate from the other is none.

As for our King I offer in his service all I have,

    up to and including my very life,

But beyond that for eternity I belong

    to the Spirit, the Father, and the Son Jesus Christ."

"Then freeze you will and burn as well.

Then see if your God sends you to Heaven or to Hell.

Of course, only half will freeze and the other half burn.

Ice and fire do not mix, but must take turns."

"As must oneness and threeness,

  I swear by the Great Gods Who are Two,"

Said the Mobed, and then he said further,

  "I offer this one last chance to you.

Recant, repent! Before half of you ends in fire

  and the other in ice.

Loyalty to One Shah of Shahs and two Great Gods

  is your freedom's price!"

"Then bring the snow from the mountain peak

  and make fire with the flint,"

Joseph commanded "And may the One True God

  forgive you for your sins.

I forgive you as you know not what you do.

While viciously cruel you are pitiably ignorant too."

The mobed screamed, "Fine that is it!

  Guards, freeze his arms and chest and burn his legs!

But leave his head, I say leave his head,

  I do not want this evil-doer too soon dead!

May he live with the pain bringing on his demise.

I want him to see his torture with his eyes."

So they burnt Joseph at one end
　　　　and froze him at the other,
Till a wondrous miracle transpired
　　　　through the intercession of the Holy Mother.
The frost and the fire spread to each other
　　　　until Joseph's body was all ice aflame,
Yet the cold did not stop his heart
　　　　nor did the heat consume his limbs in pain,

Until the mobed reached down
　　　　and drew an ornate ceremonial knife,
Raised it up, brought it down
　　　　and took martyr Joseph's life.
Joseph's body unfroze and its fire went out
　　　　at the death of this martyr blest.
His body lay without blemish or scar
　　　　except the one in his chest.

Yet the mobed at once froze and burnt his arm
Driving down the knife doing the deed of harm.
Shocked by his evil and this new sign from the Lord,
The mobed went to the palace's Christian doctor
　　　　to heal his limb (and perhaps something more).

Yom Kippur

To "atone"
    is to
Be "at one."

Be "at one,"
For thus so is
The Lord our God.

Keep That Light Alive: A Gospel Hymn for Hanukkah

Well, way back about 2200 years ago,

    There was a Greek king from Syria

    And he was a schmo.

He ruled o'er the land of the Hebrew nation

    And he thought God should take a vacation.

Well, the Lord God don't need no time off,

    So things for this king was 'bout to get rough.

He didn't know what was 'bout to go down,

    But it was gonna happen in Jerusalem town.

There was a light!

Oh, there was a light!

Runnin' on empty like an automobile,

Runnin' on nothin' but the Lord God's Will.

    The Lord God don't need no oil

    To keep that light alive.

Keep that light alive!

Oh, keep that light alive!

    The Lord God don't need no oil

    To keep that light alive.

Well, that no-good king put up in the Lord God's Temple

    An altar to Zeus;

The Jews don't got no use for Zeus,

So if you know what's good for you, you gonna vamoose.

Then the High Priest Mattathias, his sons, and others aplenty

    Started hammerin' heathens like a Jewish John Henry.

There was a light!

Oh, there was a light!

Runnin' on empty like an automobile,

Runnin' on nothin' but the Lord God's Will.

    The Lord God don't need no oil

    To keep that light alive.

Keep that light alive!

Oh, keep that light alive!

    The Lord God don't need no oil

    To keep that light alive.

Well, the Hebrew people broke through all them chains,

But they didn't forget the most important thing remains —

 To give thanks to God and to praise His Name.

So, they came to the Temple with a lamp for to light,

But there ain't enough oil to keep it burnin' right and bright.

But lit it still and — wonder of wonders from the Holy One! —

 That lamp kept burnin' like a lil' bitty sun.

There was a light!

Oh, there was a light!

Runnin' on empty like an automobile,

Runnin' on nothin' but the Lord God's Will.

 The Lord God don't need no oil

 To keep that light alive.

Keep that light alive!

Oh, keep that light alive!

 The Lord God don't need no oil

 To keep that light alive.

Well, you seen that menorah and you seen that dreidel —

> You may o' even seen 'em since you was in the cradle —

But don't forget the story and, more than that and what's best,

> Oil or no oil, light a lamp in your chest.

There is a light!

Oh, there is a light!

Runnin' on empty like an automobile,

Runnin' on nothin' but the Lord God's Will.

> The Lord God don't need no oil

> To keep that light alive.

Keep that light alive!

Oh, keep that light alive!

> The Lord God don't need no oil

> TO KEEP THAT LIGHT ALIVE!

Death's no time machine
Going back destroying life
As we once lived it.

I set with care my message
Bottled on the boundless sea.

*

No second beheads;
I must feel my stomach's blade.
Still, honor comes first.

I cannot make the temple;
I meet and kill Buddha here.

The door is narrow

And ego's immensity

Cannot fit the frame.

Leave it at the coat-check room;

Your truest friend waits within.

*

Lest I proudly preach

Humility, I preach it

Firstly to myself.

I speak not as one humble,

But as one who seeks to be.

Heaven is only other than hell

    In virtue of one's entry.

The kingdom of heaven is that of hell;

    That one same kingdom lies within.

Two gates approach the central singularity,

    One through peace and one through pain.

In each case one ends alone —

    With oneself in God

    And with God within oneself.

*

Eternal life is not my after-life

As distinct from during or before,

Or distinct as mine from yours,

But the single universal life

That timelessly endures.

I know not whether other lives

Before or after this extend.

If death is our end in time,

Still time is not our end.

It is a garment we remove,

And maybe, maybe not, re-dress.

Eternity, our nakedness,

Eternally remains unmoved.

*

My love, as now I lie upon death's door,

I know I shall find

You in God hereafter,

As I have found God in you here before.

Funeral Instructions

When ye lay me down to my last sleep,
Let lie my husk upon dried long grass lining
But a simple coffin all of wood.

Drape the Cummings tartan on the lid and lay me deep
With kilted piper piping forth Amazing Grace.

Recite the psalms and bear with thee
That though my body spoil in its grave,
Amazingly my soul shall keep.

Limits limit limits

In reciprocity of finitude;

The snake its own tail swallows.

Yet in so self-consuming,

The serpent shows a circle,

Symbol of infinity.

See the circle in the serpent

And thus see being — boundless of itself —

Being this to that and that to this,

But only ever its same self.

Wedding of the Lotus and the Rose:

A Response to Vachel Lindsay

Siddartha rises from the muck immaculate,

As Mary through the thorns comes forth unscathed.

Each board ships bearing gifts of flowers, riding waves

Upon an odyssey seeking forth in twain to meet

At a bridge of water

Spanning North and South in the New World,

Where to tie in floral knot of spirit's marriage

East and West of the Old

at the World Pole

Of Human, Earth, and Heaven.

Ready to Burst

After Pamela Benham's
Ink Painting of the Same Title

Ink	*Dancing as*
channels	*Yin and Yang*
Chi	
Into vines	*About their*
and tendrils	*original*
	enlightenment
Swirling	*In the*
in interlace	*Buddha-womb*
With the	*Of the*
crane and	*Great Ultimate*
dragon	*of the Way.*

The Rock

From Alexis Avlamis' Painting of the Same Title

In a cog in cog cosmos,

Destruction fuels production fuels destruction,

As artifacts and buildings interweave

To form a mechanical tapestry

Spreading across space

And so comprising a new night sky.

Through machines the human race

Replace

Nature and so too thus ourselves —

Or so much so

As may be

In the kingdom of the possible.

In the kingdom of the possible

There is no perpetual motion;

Its impossibility

Inevitably

Conquers the impulse for mechanical conquest.

Cogs lose force and then lose form,

    Reverting to the metals nature gave them,

Then to accept

Anew, as again

Nature gives shapes and motions.

Nature gives shapes and motions

    Of utter simplicity to the soul,

      Thus

      Utterly precluding

Full and irreversible absorption

To its Promethean attachments.

The soul's metal is prior to the forms and forces

      It takes on

    And ultimately takes off.

We are ever still the spear-hunter

Stalking out the stars

Of whose dust we came

And will return to

Before and after

We have lived

In a cog in cog cosmos.

Sunflower 2

From Cathy Ganschinietz's
Watercolor of the Same Title

A sunflower's circling bursts of yellow hue

Match shape and color with the orb of flame

To which all growing creatures' lives are due

And from which sunflowers specially take their name.

As flowers come, so too the sun first came

By flowering forth its form in matter's space.

Its form is Euclid's circle, extant frame

Without beginning, ever set in place.

The circle's timeless birth to form its face

Occurs as parent point's fresh radii

In all directions equal distance race

To weld circumference, crown of majesty.

From seed of perfect oneness cosmos sprouts

With suns and flowers circling about.

Carousel

> *From Rosalinda Post-Lucas'*
> *Watercolor of the Same Title*

A child's whimsical plaything

 Bespeaks the cosmic Play,

As beneath the pony's fragile paper

  Drives a mythic steed's strong truth

  Charging through vivid color patterns

  In circles of eternity.

Look with sage's mind

  Through child's eyes

And ride ye forth

  Past the mobs of humdrum naysayers

  Smugly chained in shadow-caves.

Ride ye into faierie queenedoms

  More real than disbelief's delusions.

Remembering the Kiss

From Felicia Olin's Painting of the Same Title

Klimt caught a single instant

    Set in isolation,

    Seceding from

    Time's ontological inferno.

With vision's brush he deftly wrought

A golden icon

    Of a love

Holy if not Christian,

    Not per se,

    And yet so very

        Christlike —

An icon from Byzantium,

    Of Yeats

    If not of

        Chrysostom.

Olin echoes Klimt's new art,

    Indeed throughout her oeuvre,

Though here in reference to his *Kiss*,

    His of bliss, hers of wist.

Nostalgia swirls up with tree-limbs

    And with tresses red

    As though Burne-Jones

    Had seen them with his mind's eye.

Olin, too, thus snares a solitary moment,

    Freeing it of fetters

    With which time encumbers,

Now none but eternal now

As with — one with — Klimt's.

Cosmic Wheel

From Wendy Allen's Fabric Art Piece of the Same Title

As the wise hymn time

    Eternity's image

    Set in motion,

So too the wheel is to the circle,

    With its clockwise or

    Reverse rotation,

The sun in sequence

Rises, sets, and rises

    Ad infinitum,

    Ab inifinitum,

    To and from,

    Sub specie aeternitatis —

The sun the icon of the One,

    The sun's own sun,

    Shams-al-shams

    As Persian poets say.

Our sun is one of countless suns

    Wheeling in a dervish dance

    Through endless space—

    Order out of chaos out of oneness.

In the jeweled-silk circle motion crossing through the cosmos,

The one many made of many ones

              Hymns *the* One—

    From one, to one, in one,

    Ab unum, ad unum, in unum,

    Al-Ahad,

    The One.

Astronomy Domine

From Janet Sgro's Painting of the Same Title

Gleaming orbs arise,

Glowing forth glittering luminescence

Across uncomprehending darkness;

The circle clusters

Spiral,

Swoop,

And swirl,

As they

Hurl,

Hurl,

Hurl

Radiant iridescence to reverberate

Glassy porcelain flicker-flames.

They make music showing chords

And contrapuntal crab-crawls,

      Along with other inversions

      Developing one omni-varied theme

      Through warp and weft,

Weaving notes light as light past

            Vertical and horizontal parallels

      Criss-Crossing pages

         Of the universal hymn-book.

Cycling angel-dance emerges,

      Traversing cosmic space

      Through time

— As the moving icon of eternity.

Babel

From Katherine Pippin Pauley's Sculpture of the Same Title

The pinnacle of human hubris seeks

To storm Saint Peter's gate by force of arms.

That then on God's own throne atop our peaks

We take our seats to spread our cruelty's harms,

In service of our ego-beast—the one

Perpetual idol with its host of charms.

The inner Moloch leaks its sludge to run,

To seek out lowest levels through great ages

And through its flood of filth supplant the sun.

Its slaves span tales in Hebrew-lettered pages,

Oil canvases by Breughel, cinema

By Lang; no less in history it rages.

Ape-self, deformed by spurning offered reason,

Scales ever higher after might and mammon.

And yet this climb looks upward bound but by
Distortion plaguing our perception's grasp,
Reversing all directions in a lie.

The more the ego climbs it falls, at last
Then falling next to nil; the more that *you*
Are then the less you *are*. Your ego cast

Your Being down until you break in two,
And two again, and so on and so forth,
Until your selfishness robs self from you.

Hence It is better to instead recall
The Sufi dictum that in bowing to
The ground one looks downward from God's Throne-Hall.
The less *you* are the more you *are* — not you
But God in you and you in turn in The True.

FORECOURT

Grim-visaged great chiefs,

   grey bearded heroes,

Brood over brew cups,

   bread, and roasted meat,

Mining depths of memory,

   missing long since past

Days bright with fell daring,

   doing great and mighty feats

Seeking, by their sword-craft,

   such fine prizes of

Red gold, red blood, and

   red-tressed maidens

As all, even mortal foes, must

   acknowledge to be glorious.

More than one among their throng

   make claim of having slain a dragon.

Now though, of these nail-iron men,

   none there are but that

Regret and rue the creeping

   rust of old age.

Acts of Intolerance

From Preston Jackson's Sculpture of the Same Title

A dirge hums, almost numb,

Among

Survivors

Groping through the rubble of their lives.

When

Then

A sudden burning gold-spark flash

Upon a desolate field of ash

Announces the arrival

Of the phoenix's renewal.

From the blaze

Come the blues

Filled with mutes

Not of silence

But of horns getting gutbucket growls

Roaring forth the syncopated march

Of a people's newfound advancement.

Prairie Sumac

From an Art Glass Window at
Frank Lloyd Wright's Dana Thomas House

Lead caming leads glass of amber-gold

Into angles as they arch and branch

And dangle these rigid ribbons

Shimmering in parallel.

How else would Nature grow

           A window

From straight lines as seeds?

The Rajput Stallion

From Terri Zee's Mosaic Sculpture

Proudly bearing in endurance,

Long and far,

Long and far,

Mid the Thar,

The scorching hot

Thar desert,

Land of Rajahs,

Rides this steed,

The mount of Rajahs,

Warrior kings renowned

For martial valor,

Skill, and   splendor.

Though far, so far,

Out mid the Thar,

Come soon the steed will re-ascend the hill-fort,

There to meet anew with princely pomp

The neighbor kings and Mughal envoys,

So too those

Come from

Deccani courts.

All fill pleasure palace garden grounds.

All will watch

As row past marching row stride past,

All set in multi-colored

Persian patterned silks abundantly bejeweled.

Quartet

Cross-Rhythm — Isorhythm — Counterpoint — Culmination

x x X X x X x X X x x X
x x X X x X x X X x x X

x x X x a X x x X a x X x x A
x x X x a X x x X a x X x x A
x x X x a X x x X a x X x x A

x X x X a X b X
x A x X x B a X
x X x A b X x X
a X x B x A x X

x x X X a X b X
X a x X x b A X
x X x A B x x X
a x X B x A x X

From the shores lining Congo, drums beat out a THREE—

Against FOUR coming forth from drums Niger-way. BOOM!

Guillaume de Machaut set his fine lines so that melodies grow

In such times that go pacing at rate slower, faster than go

Rhythms beating row past subsequent row again to and fro.

With J.S. Bach's notes set in lines,

He wove across these thin rows others,

Like—although different from—them,

So that lace trim arose atop.

From these great welling floods flows new,

Lush interlace. Jazz grows, *swims*.

Modern music hits tones likewise weaving.

And thus so the circle turns.

Latin Practice

Practicing romance,
I suggest conjugating;
　　　She in turn declines.

*

Haiku

I would hurt no one,
Yet crane my neck for train wrecks.
　　　Monster by proxy?

*

Canadian Haiku

A moose drinking Crown
Beneath a flame red maple —
　　　What is it a-boot?

Haiku for Thea Chesley

Veteran huntress,
Grizzled, white-locked lioness,
Not just boys have manes.

*

Ah Thea

Ah, Thea!
　　　Divinest disbeliever,
You know not what you do —
　　　Namely,

　　　God's work.

Russillo, our Rat Pack Rossini,

Operatic bass of blues and standards,

Blowing harp with heart.

***

Hark!

Mark,

The noble, no-bull, evangelist

Of a left and forward social gospel,

Winged lion

Tall, fur-flagged tail

Feathery flight regal as eagle,

Workingman's superman seeking

To impede a greed stampede

Of plutocratic pachyderms,

A labor of love born of a love of labor,

Bleeding heart better than all heartless

Beasts who bleed poor people

Dry past every drop.

Mark, though I may mark our differing —

Comparing merits

Twixt a green holy fool martyr

And a jackass battleaxe hawk,

Or over shielding conscience

In its concern for life's first bloom —

All told I admire you

And find uncommon honor

Fighting a common foe

Alongside such a workers' warrior.

Pie-Man Arch

Simple Simon met a pie-man.

Pie-man Arch told this Simon

Of a local open mic.

As our Simon know that rhyme 'n

Meter met his like,

He thought attending might be nice.

Wednesday night found Simon climb in

His auto and drive down

To the prettiest, oldest part of town,

Where at Robbie's he could dine in

And enjoy some wine 'n pie in

Enjoyment of poetic sound.

Defenestration

Overton makes windows
Right, left, high, and low.
I've been thrown through
Enough to know.

"Congolium"?

A source of — or force for — profuse confusion

Until realizing its role as allusion

To Conger's rising, lilting conga line of rollicking verse.

Verbiage, ranging from Vachel

(Lindsay's longest, the Congo, suits Conger)

To the bovine arrival,

      Sent in to strains of ekphrastic abstraction,

Elicits lucid, raw, emphatic reaction.

A prairie Da Vinci polymath

In a Josephite polychrome coat,

Conger — wisdom upon his whiskers —

Soars with film to catch the path

Of aerial, ironclad dragonflies whizzing

Into moments of immobile suddenness

Now on small yet sturdy mailable paper slabs

Or bedecking walls and halls of a humble museum.

Why not "congolium"?

Chemistry alone remains for his resume.

"Congolium"?

(Revised Standard Version)

A confusing term, until I find

It refers to Conger's poetic lines.

From Vachel Lindsay's long poem "Congo,"

To sending in cows with an abstract song,

All excites a rise in the listener.

A local renaissance man—

Wearing a patchwork sport jacket

And a beard befitting his wisdom—

Flies and snaps pictures of planes,

Placing the photographs on postcards

And perhaps his museum wall.

Why not "congolium"?

Chemistry alone remains for his resume.

Donald Trump's Christmas Carol:
An Unfinished Tale in Verse

Donald Trump's dad was dead as a doornail
      the day he appeared on Trump's door.
"Oh, dear old dad, things have gone bad —
      but it's nothing more money won't fix.
Things now are sore, but more money will fix it;
      so, please sir, I want some more."

"Come inside, son, and see my full form.
      My money bought these binding chains!
I come here to give, not money, but hope of a pardon,
      a pardon while time still remains."

"The power of pardon is *my* prerogative!
      Why would I need one from *you*?
With the stroke of a pen I can pardon myself
      and there's not a thing Muller can do.
You disloyal traitor, you turncoat like Cohen,
      no pardons for you or your crew!"

"Your power as president issuing pardons

      ends at the doorstep of death.

What's more, it won't work with the State of New York,

      but here I confess I digress.

A set of three spirits are set to show visions

      which you then may use to reform."

"Invaders incoming! Illegals no doubt —

      which is why we must build us a wall.

Now go on back home, just leave me alone,

      and never again come to call."

The first ghost came visiting later that night

      and entered Trump's sight,

Who now hoped that this might

      not be such a blight,

As this ghost looked so old

      and so too looked so white,

Until Trump took a bump

      and flew fast to the past through the night . . .

I saw Freckle licking Santa Claus,

Yelping loud

And bouncing on him, too.

She acts like we don't feed her,

And asks if he might need her,

And if he'll feed her lots of treats

And fun-fun food.

I saw Freckle licking Santa Claus

Last night.

You deserve love,

Just not the love

I have.

You have so much good in you,

But I only love you

For the ways you're bad.

I hate that I love you

For all the wrong reasons.

Nevermore She Calls Me by My Name

      From David Allan Poe

      and Edgar Allan Coe

Once upon a midnight trying

All I could do to keep from crying,

Feeling — as sometimes I do —

'Tis useless to remain . . .

No need my darling call me darling,

Though nevermore she calls me by my name.

She need never call me Waylon Jennings,

Nor need she call me Charlie Pride,

Nor even Merle Haggard — Nevermore!

Though I be on her fighting side.

      I keep my place so long as she permits.

      Dispassionate I linger in the rain.

      No need my darling call me darling,

      Though nevermore she calls me by my name.

I see my name's listing in her ledger

And upon marquees of venues where I play,

Though but one time I know —

>> When final trumpets blow —

Only then my name rings loud upon that Day.

>> I keep my place so long as she permits.

>> Dispassionate I linger in the rain.

>> No need my darling call me darling,

>> Though nevermore she calls me by my name.

I was deep in drink the day that came my mother's pardon.

Even so I sought to fetch her in the rain.

Yet ere my carriage's arrival at the station

She fell victim to a locomotive train.

>> I keep my place so long as she permits.

>> Dispassionate I linger in the rain.

>> No need my darling call me darling,

>> Though nevermore she calls me by my name.

Springfield's Own

(Parody of Rolling Stone)

Well, I am a local poet

With a three-ring binder's worth of verse to show it;

I'm a regular at the local open mic.

I rhyme about beauty and I rhyme about truth

But I made more money as a kid every time I lost a tooth.

So you can just imagine when I saw it on the page as proof

I was in the middle of Springfield's Own!

Springfield's Own!

Springfield's Own!

Yes, that's the real me and not some other!

Gotta get an extra copy for my mother!

Springfield's Own!

Springfield's Own!

I ain't gettin' richer,

But at least I got my picture

In the middle of

Springfield's Own!

Well, we got a harp-blowin' crooner,

Though he would sooner

Recite to you

Political haiku.

While Will will take a skillet to your brain

Reading from Anthony Bourdain

And Blake's mythologies and parodies

Will leave you never quite the same.

A bearded elder statesman

Reads Vachel, 'cause he's a great man.

Yet even amidst all these talented friends to me,

I never thought I'd live to see

My picture in the middle of Springfield's Own!

Springfield's Own!

Springfield's Own!

Yes, that's the real me and not some other!

Gotta get an extra copy for my mother!

Springfield's Own!

Springfield's Own!

I ain't getting' richer,

But at least I got my picture

In the middle of

Springfield's Own!

Maid's Song

I serve a lady
As a maid.
For what's to be
My plans are laid;
For now at least
I'm gettin' paid.

Not too long and you will see
A boy come from the old country
Will call on me
  Call on me
Come callin' for to marry
  For to marry me.
Then no more a maid
But a wife I'll be.

We'll dance a jig,

And pour a jug,

And drink us each

A great big slug

That day we wed

  Day we wed

With a weddin' full

O' guests well fed.

Go Kentucky

That bad girl burned my heart

Like the black alligator char

From a Wild Turkey bourbon whiskey barrel.

Now I'm back here at home,

In a place I've always known,

Clean away from that witch-queen Miss Carol.

I will follow the wild turkey

On down to knob creek.

I'll be drunk in three hours,

My old self in a week.

The Grass is bluer on the other side

Of the Mason-Dixon line.

Double barrel shotgun and

Single barrel whiskey,

It's time for me

To go Kentucky.

Away from hard worries

And far from fast hurries,

I'll set myself deep in my chair.

With a glass in my hand

I'll be a new man

With time enough to spare.

I will follow the wild turkey

On down to knob creek.

I'll be drunk in three hours,

My old self in a week.

The Grass is bluer on the other side

Of the Mason-Dixon line.

Double barrel shotgun and

Single barrel whiskey,

It's time for me

To go Kentucky.

McFarland Blues

I ain't seen my darlin'
Since they sent me down to McFarland
    And they won't even let me drink whisky.
I can't drink no whisky
And when I feel frisky
    My baby ain't here to fool 'round.

If I weren't crazy before
    They shoved me in through the door,
Now — no booze and no whores —
    I'm stone crazy straight to the core.

My woman done left me at Christmas,

> And my tree lights sure have dimmed.

Woman left me at Christmas,

> Them tree lights sure have dimmed.

But ain't nobody found not even a minute

To say, "too bad, too bad, too bad, poor ol' Jim."

Well I since found me another woman

> And my nose sure been glowin' red.

Yes I found this here my new woman

> And she got my nose shinin' all nice 'n red.

We get up 'n check the stockin';

Then we set ourselves back down to bed.

That ol' woman tried crawlin' back at New Year's,

> After she didn't get nothin' but a lump o' coal.

She crawled on back come New Year's Day

> After findin' her sock ain't got nothin' but coal.

Well, I don't got no time for none o' 'dat

Cuz 'dese days I'm just too damn old.

Jimmy Jam Jamboree

My name is James,
And my daddy is Jim.
I grew up as Jamie
To be clear
Who's me and who's him.

Oh girl, I want it clear
For you to see
That I would be
Happy to be
Your Jimmy Jam Jamboree.

Some folks like
To go the fair.
They like festivals,
Carnivals,
They think it's all
Wonderful.

I think it'd be

    Wonderful

    Girl

For you to see

    That I would be

    Happy to be

Your Jimmy Jam Jamboree.

Some like marmalade,

Others like jelly,

Anything sweet

To put deep down

In your belly.

I got for you,

Oh miss ma'am,

The very sweetest

Sort of jam.

    Oh girl, I want you to see

    That I would be

    Happy to be

    Your Jimmy Jam Jamboree.

Lil' Houseboy Blues

I'll pour my syrup on yo' hotcakes,
      Put my stick o' butter on yo' bread.
Pour that sweet, sweet syrup on yo' hotcakes,
      Put that big ol' stick o' butter
      All 'cross yo' loaves of bread.

I'm gonna go turn up yo' furnace
      And then I'll come . . .
      and I'll turn down yo' bed.

I wanna be your lil' houseboy, pretty mama,
      So leave yo' back do' open fo' me!

I'll deliver cream straight to yo' winda'
      'N bring my block o' ice
      To keep yo' jelly roll fresh.
I'll deliver thick, heavy cream to yo' winda'
      'N ya know my block o' ice
      Will keep yo' jelly roll nice 'n fresh fresh.

We can play stick and balls in the back yard
      Or like your dog I'll take my stick
      And play fetch.

I wanna be your lil' houseboy, pretty mama,

So leave yo' back do' open fo' me!

I wanna be your lil' houseboy, pretty mama,

So leave yo' back do' open fo' me.

I'll let myself right on in

'N see to everythin' mama needs.

I'll be your lil' houseboy, pretty mama,

Just leave yo' back do' open fo' me!

Dirge Blues

I

(to a bluesed-out rendition
of Chopin's Funeral March)

They say pray for the dead,

And the dead will pray for you.

They say pray for the dead,

And the dead will pray for you.

Well, sometimes no one left alive

Will lift a finger,

So that's what you gotta do.

II

(to a bluesed-out rendition
of Bach's Toccata and Fugue in D Minor)

Well, I see death

Just there a'comin' around the bend.

Well, I see death

Just there a'comin' around the bend.

Well, I don't mind if death

Is comin' for me,

'Cause he's

Just takin' me back to my friends.

III

(back to Chopin's Funeral March)

They say pray for the dead,

    And the dead will pray for you.

They say pray for the dead,

    And the dead will pray for you.

And then when I myself am dead,

    I'll then be free of these

    No-good livin' fools.

I'm gonna stew me up a chicken leg,

    And boil me up a pot o' rice.

I'm gonna stew me up a chicken leg,

    And boil me up a pot o' rice.

    I know I'll be feelin' hungry,

    So this here oughta be pretty nice.

I'll put spice and veggies with the chicken,

    Add in some butter, cream, and oil.

I'll put spice and veggies with the chicken,

    Add in some butter, cream, and oil.

    Then I'll let it all set

    When it's done with the boil.

I'll pour it in on the rice,

    And then I'll be ready to sup.

I'll pour it in on the rice,

    And then I'll be ready to sup.

    I'll scarf it on down,

    Crack open a beer, and then—bottoms up!

Mean Ol' Mister Schoolmaster Blues

Oh mister schoolmaster,

>   Why you treat me so bad this way?

Oh, mean ol' mister schoolmaster,

>   Why you treat me like a low down dirty dog this way?

>   Recess, you set them bullies out pickin' on me,

>   So I don't even get no time to play.

Oh, but I'm the one gets in trouble,

>   not the bullies pickin' on me.

Oh, yes, I'm the one you always punish,

>   not all them mean, nasty bullies pickin' on me!

>   You say you ain't seen 'em do it;

>   You only see what you wanna see.

You say you demand respect.

 Well, give it here 'n I'll give it right on back.

You talk 'bout me owin' you respect.

 Well, give it here 'n I'll pay it right on back.

 Till that day come, mister schoolmaster,

 I can't give what I ain't never had.

Missin' Rain Blues

> (to the tune of Skip James'
> "Hard Time Killin' Floor Blues")

You had a name
But weren't for me to know.
Just all the same
I hate to see you go.

It ain't the same
Since you don't show no mo'.
Lawd, I miss the rain
And now I curse the snow.

It's a damned old shame
And that's for sho'.
Went hard as you came,
You didn't go down slow.

After trouble and pain
And walkin' out that do',
There gonna always remain
That same old amber glow.

You was your mama's
Bad lil' child,
But you was wise
As you was wild.

Went to Japan,
Went to Paree,
You done seen all
There was to see.

You shook your stuff
And you sung your song.
Can somethin' so good
Last too long?

You rode your hoss
And you rode it well,
Kept on ridin'
No matter you fell.

Some didn't like
What all you did,
But you was too proud
To keep it hid.

You led a sportin' life,
But that don't mean
You was any less lady
Than a pure bred queen.

You was dirty
And you was smart,
Took that jelly roll
And made it art.

Don't know if you hurt
When you died,
But I hurt like hell
When I found out and cried.

First I heard you was gone
I thought it some mean joke.
When I knew it was true
It felt like a choke.

You was nasty
But you was nice,
Good lookin' bad girl
Still treatin' folks right.

Flowers For You, Cat

From Rosalinda Post-Lucas'
Watercolor of the Same Title

Angel, is them flowers sweet

    Up by rainbow bridge?

Is them flowers sweet as you

    Way up by rainbow bridge?

I'm in the valley of the shadow

    And you way up past that ridge.

Your folks done called you home;

    You was booked and got to go.

Folks was callin' you home;

    You was booked and bound to go.

I'll meet you right by them flowers

    When they lay me six feet low.

When I leave,

    I leave

    My heart behind

    Until I come again—

But I leave it with assurance

        That you lock it safely

        In your jewel-case mind

            Behind

    Your emerald eyes.

My perfect holy boy

In snow silk coat

Pierces my Teresian heart

With blue eyes as sharp

In love as angels' arrows.

He climbs upon my chest,

Seeking entry to warmth and union.

I welcome him with emptiness of self,

Opening a Marian womb

To carry the holy boy's love

And bear it to the world.

Rama

From pewter thread striped

    Prince coat

Flowing over snow-sheen silk

    (as of his late brother

    buried since in state)

Scepter willow limbs descend

    In ballet grace

As ivory dagger sets gesticulate,

        Radiate

Mudras of affection.

Kitten Romp in Candy Land

Just like a ball of cotton candy there, sir.
Yes, good sir, a bouncy ball
        of sunshine orange cotton candy —
Fluffy rocketing firework
        of mad sparkling sweet sprinkles
Igniting, delighting, inviting to frolic
Amidst pastel powdered sugar clouds
        of Easter rainbows
Springing from gold-pots
        of shiny emerald candy coins.

For Zack and Lauren's First Anniversary

As with East and West
Each being what it is
By virtue of the other,

So too with your union
By your bond
Differences define
One love free from bound.

On My Mother Turning Fifty Four Graceful Years

I hope you will excuse if I consult the muse,

Muffin's and Minou's

Most sacred servant serving rhyme,

As now at such a time

Writing you, I hope to choose

The words that may prove best to use.

Compose an ode, a sonnet, a ghazal, a blues?

Paint a tone-picture in whatsoever verbal hues

As may best extend, such as I so eagerly intend,

My gratitude without end

And my likewise boundless mirth

On this day of yours, my mother's, birth.

At twenty-two you dropped me down and brought me in

My earthly journey to begin, with guidance from my kin, that I

might win

Enlightenment.

Nine months and thirty one years,

Pain, blues, agony, blood, sweat, and tears

(Though, on balance, more dear have been the cheers)

You have nurtured me and helped me steer

Past crippling fear, till now here

I peer into myself; I see the structure clear

Of all—him and her, they, we, it (whatever it may be)

All one, not separately.

I love you as myself for you ARE me (that is, ultimately).

Distinctions are but garmemts the Self takes on and off,

I the garment you cut from *your* cloth.

Please think not so, that I fail to know

The sacrifices—so great, so many, oh!—

You made that you could sew the stitches of richest

Embroidery

Upon your seamstress' mistresspiece.

You the artist, I the autist . . . ic swatch,

Your cloth, without sloth you watch

Testing the unending, unbending patience

     Of your needling hand

Well, to tell the truth, bent it has, but break it never will,

Whatever my inadvertent ill, owling lecture, or clumsy spill,

You have your fill, it seems until,

     You might wonder if I am off my pills

Yet even as the mood may chill, it fails kill

Our bond, more than mere thrill, it endures alike through Storm

and still.

I hope I may be wise, wise enough to realize

You are more than spy my eyes.

Yes, I am the guy and you are the guy's,

But you are firstly yours.

I see you through my lens, a lens with limits —

Oh, the lens' limits limit not my love,

'Tis a rosy lens!

(Thorns but verify it is a true, living rose).

Even then this goes.

What remains, drains, once sun melts the snow,

Revealing but the spare, bare Ground below.

This, in turn, is none but the surface of the sun.

Seeing into my center, all is One.

We are the same inner perfection,

Our distinct identities but reflection,

Of the singular Self.

Seeing you as mine I know not you as yours,

Yet seeing you as me and us as all and all as One

I know no greater honor I could have won

Than to be yours – God's - Son.

Even as I at thirty one

Congratulate you on turning fifty-four,

Please know you (we! all!) are without limit more

Than time can store or pour

From one year to another.

Space too can race from place to place

Without beginning to truly trace

The root of our reality — Reality Itself, the only really Real.

On My Two Mothers' Two Marriages

A union of two houses

    Already long since one

Under God's Church through

    Apostolic succession.

Let no man tear asunder

    What together God hath joined.

If that man be Caesar,

    Such is beside the point.

Render under Caesar his,

    But his is not to wed.

But only to acknowledge

    Spouses' vows instead.

Here was not the Church

    Lording over the state,

But state spurning Church's union

    Of two women mates.

Commiseration

Here I am now, not quite drunk —
      Yet more so, though, than is my wont —
And more so then again beside,
As from my friends I've imbibed
Their sorrows such now mine.

From friendship friend's life is friend's alike;
Strong ale serves as but a chaser.

Immortalized in bronzer,

Her hair could not be blonder,

>And it has that photogenic sheen.

She's a shampoo commercial girl

>Coming out a TV screen.

She's a prefabulastic

>Cookie-cutter

>Coke-whore

>Queen.

Jurisprudence

Gavel, gavel!

Order 'mongst the rabble!

Justice is swift and 'tis fair.

Seek ye your prize,

Yet please realize,

Cheating's not brooked here.

So beware!

Pindaric Ode

In a race for three to win

Three have won—the three who'd run,

Needful task all others shun.

When alone among who may

Three steel souls dare venture forth,

Participation's proof of worth.

Hail the venturing fine heroes here among us—

These our Jason, brave Ulysses, and Aeneas!

Sunrise August 2, 2013

A pink and purple sunrise

    comes over my building of brick red;

Verdant green courtyard trees

    glow dimly in the day's new light.

I put this scene to writing fast I could,

    but the sky's already dull blue.

Enjoy the sunrise as you can,

    though it does not rise for you.

Shakespearean Vaudeville

A: Ho, good fellow! Come whence ye and upon what business?

B: From our good butcher's bring I forth fair new provisions as well fit the fair new bride awaiting at my door.

A: Joy meet ye both! Tis fit and fair a new provider provide fit fare fit for one so fair and fit. As thou sayest tis the "good butcher," trust I aright thy new bought fare tis meet and not foul?

B: Nay, tis fowl and not meat.

A: I grieve to hear it.

B: Whence thy grief? Found I never grief from goose nor capon save as followed excess in their joy!

A: Ah, I take now thy intent aright! Tis not foul meat but fair fowl.

B: Aye, the good butcher's fowl tis meet as tis his meat likewise.

A: Then must I acquaint thy butcher with mine purse. Find I till now meat and fowl visiting the fair. Only the meat tis not meet and the fowl tis most foul.

B: Fair such fair tis not!

A: Nay, tis a fowl fair for the fair's fare is fowl, foul fowl and foul meat, an unfair fair not meet for meat nor for meeting.

B: Now, fine friend, to meet was meet though I must hie hence anon with good butcher's meet fowl to meet fair bride lest I meet foul and good bride a butcher be.

The Requisite Etiquette in Connecticut

The matter of manners

In Massachusetts

May such surfeit permit

As the requisite etiquette

In Connecticut

So very severely forbids.

Whereas writing songs

Puts words to music

So as then to sing the words,

Writing poetry

Puts music IN the words

So that the words themselves may sing.

Upon the Occasion of an Angel's Flight

Within each volume lies latent
Waiting an entire world
Ready upon a reader's gaze
To commence its cosmogenesis.

Neatly nestling row on row, shelf on shelf,
These worlds whirl within a broader multiverse;
You, the high presiding angel, aptly administer
These, the Divine Mind's abundant manifestations.

Ode to Keats

Though our physician could not heal himself,

His sharp and gleaming metal implements

No use, he heals us when from off our shelf

We take and read the verses he invents

In gold-bound pages like he loved from Homer.

He salves with fragrant balm our souls. Hellenic

And chivalric legends live in verbal

gem-set icons. Odes and sonnets lower

To our mortal sight verities cosmic,

Celestial, intelligible.

Though living barely but to be a man,

He lives in death like kings of legend, stone-

Entombed in Plato's solids. Tennyson and

The Brotherhood as pilgrims sigh and moan

And make oblation, as he they venerate

Had made to Spenser, Milton and the bard.

Though he's since joined his late young brother, living

With his timeless peers past mortal state,

Now we in turn must wait and hold our part

As did his dear bereaved betrothed surviving.

Rhyme Royal

When in the second Richard's reign the court
Life briefly triumphed over battle's death,
Not but a generation past *grand mort*,
From France and Italy he brought fresh breath,
With pageantry and finery, till theft
Brought back war's ruin to the ruling throne,
Eclipsing sun that briefly, brightly shone.

Italian Sonnet

A new life dawns in Tuscany's trecento.

French cathedral craft and courtly love,

With Eastern goods from Venice, push and shove

Through Sienna, Florence, Orvieto.

The friars and the merchant princes pay

For artists to compose, sculpt, paint — to *pray*

Through beauty to its first exemplar cause

Perfecting through His grace all nature's laws.

Then comes the Black Death. Divine comedy

Descends to hell. Hardly half are left alive.

Those left lock up like bees shut in their hive.

Some take turns telling tales in company,

All as a way of waiting patiently,

Next century to see the next new birth arrive.

ALPHABETICAL INDEX OF POEMS

Made in the USA
Coppell, TX
06 July 2021